TOWARDS A MIDDLE SYSTEM OF LAW

TOWARDS A MIDDLE SYSTEM OF LAW

David Tench

Consumers' Association
publishers of **Which?**
14 Buckingham Street
London WC2N 6DS

ISBN 0 85202 214 X
and 0 340 28163 4

Photoset by Paston Press, Norwich
Printed in England

Contents

What's this all about?

There are crimes. They are all about punishing wickedness. And there are rights. They are all about getting what you are entitled to. Crimes and rights together comprise the law.

Nowadays practically anything can be a crime. The statute book consists of thousands of things which Parliament has decided to prohibit, for one reason or another. Each year they add a lot more. It is debatable whether some of these things need to be forbidden at all. That is another argument. But is it really necessary always to make a crime of something that has to be prohibited or controlled, saying it is a crime if you don't comply? What else could be done? The answer, at the moment, is nothing. Either it is a crime or it is legal.

The idea with a middle system of law would be to regulate some matters without making them criminal. These are the things which need regulating but which most people would not consider to be wicked. Not criminal, that is, in the way that murder, theft and fraud are obviously wicked and criminal.

Much of road traffic law is regulatory in this way. Does it have to be a crime to park on a yellow line or to display a car licence in the wrong corner of your windscreen? Nearly every branch of the law—company law, employment law, consumer law, education law and so on—contains a whole host of regulatory offences of this kind. Need all of them be crimes?

If these—or some of them—ceased to be crimes, what would they be? They would become infringements or contraventions or transgressions of a new legal system—the middle system of law. In future, people who broke this type of law would be liable to a civil penalty, instead of a fine or imprisonment under the criminal law.

It surely is ridiculous for Parliament to go on legislating to make things crimes which no civilised individual really regards as criminal. It makes the law look silly. It debases the coinage of the criminal law. It adds greatly to the expense and bureaucracy of enforcing the law.

There would be great advantages if part of the criminal law were transferred to the new middle system of law. Motorists and businessmen, for example, would continue to be required to obey the law, as now, but they would not have to be investigated, prosecuted, convicted and punished as criminals for technical infringements of the law. In the majority of cases, where there is no dispute about the facts, cases would be disposed of without going to court.

Civil penalties could be fixed, or in some cases negotiated, and paid by agreement, so that the whole business could be managed with the minimum of fuss, delay and cost.

There are bits of the civil law which could also be treated by the middle system of law. Race relations and sex discrimination are largely controlled by civil law rules at the moment. They would have more teeth if infringements were made subject to civil penalties under the middle system of law.

Civil penalties already exist in tax law. The middle system of law would extend, to other branches of the law, the principles used successfully for many years in tax law.

Developing a middle system of law would give Parliament an additional option when legislating. It would be entirely up to them whether they used it, and if so what for, and in what way.

Introduction

English law comprises the criminal law and the civil law. The criminal law forbids behaviour which is harmful or a threat to the community: murder, robbery, rape, theft and many other anti-social acts. The criminal law works by imposing punishment on offenders. The civil law confers rights on individuals, and regulates their dealings and relationships within society.

The criminal law and the civil law are separately administered under the English legal system: the Crown Court and magistrates courts administer the criminal law, and the High Court and county courts administer the civil law. The result of this separate adminis-tration is that the two legal systems are kept conceptually distinct in our law. When Parliament decides to take legislative action to right a wrong, it has to decide how to do so within the framework of these separate legal systems. Behaviour requiring legislative control has to be forbidden, subject to the sanction of imprisonment or fine, under the criminal law; or made the subject of rights and obligations with the sanction of damages and injunction (coupled with the threat of imprisonment for contempt of court) under the civil law.

There is now a case for Parliament to recognise the need for a third legal system, functioning between the existing criminal and civil systems, which would have as its object the regulation of behaviour which has to be controlled, but which is not wrongful enough to merit prohibition under the criminal law.

Every year Parliament passes a number of statutes of a regulatory character, which create criminal offences. Many of these lack the traditional character of criminal law—the control of wicked behaviour in society. In addition, in recent times Parliament has resorted occasionally to the civil law to provide a somewhat con-trived system of control for behaviour which it feels cannot be made subject to criminal sanctions.

There is now a considerable body of law covering this middle ground between the pure criminal law and the pure civil law, which should be brought together and rationalised into a middle system of law. The primary sanction would be a civil penalty. In what follows, the present areas covered by this middle ground, and at present forming part of the criminal and civil law, will be examined, and the principle put forward on which the suggested middle system of law should be recognised, nurtured and developed.

Criminal law

A crime, says the Shorter Oxford English Dictionary, is

"an act punishable by law, as being forbidden by statute or injurious to the
public welfare; . . . an evil or injurious act; . . . a grave offence, a sin; a
wrong-doing".

Halsbury's Laws of England (4th edition), volume 11, para 1,
says:

"Ordinarily a crime is a wrong which affects the security or well-being of
the public generally so that the public has an interest in its suppression. A
crime is frequently a moral wrong in that it amounts to conduct which is
inimical to the general moral sense of the community. It is, however, possible to instance many crimes which exhibit neither of the foregoing
characteristics. An act may be made criminal by Parliament simply
because it is criminal process, rather than civil, which offers the more
effective means of controlling the conduct in question."

The essence of crime is that it is met with punishment. The law
determines what conduct ought to be forbidden, forbids it, and
decrees that offenders should be punished by the courts.

Strict liability

In modern times, as society had become more complex, more areas
of behaviour have become regulated by law. Nearly every statute
passed by Parliament includes sanctions for the enforcement of the
rules it enacts.

Statutes frequently create criminal offences of behaviour which
few people would really regard as criminal, of conduct for which no
criminal intent is required, and where no real element of wickedness
is involved.

In the last 100 years, there has been an immense growth in the use
of absolute offences, or offences of strict liability, that is those
where no criminal intention (*mens rea*) is needed. This is because in
some fields—for example, where health and safety of workers or
consumers is involved—Parliament has considered compliance with
standards so important that only strict compliance is adequate.

The acceptance in our system that there could be offences of strict
liability where no criminal intention is present goes back over 130
years. But since the 1950's the role of offences of strict liability in
our law has been increasingly questioned.

Mens rea

Offences involving strict liability have consistently been treated with caution by the courts. Mr Justice Wright in *Sherras v De Rutzen* in 1895 said:

> "There is a presumption that *mens rea*, an evil intention, or knowledge of the wrongfulness of the act, is an essential ingredient in every offence; but that presumption is liable to be displaced either by the words of the statute creating the offence or by the subject matter with which it deals, and both must be considered."

The judge went on to say that strict liability is imposed only in a few types of case, which include acts which are **'not criminal in any real sense'**, but are prohibited in the public interest under a penalty.

Lord Reid—in two of the significant cases on strict liability in recent times, *Warner v Metropolitan Police Commissioner* (1968) and *Sweet v Parsley* (1970), distinguished between 'quasi-criminal offences' and 'offences involving the disgrace of criminality'. In *Sweet v Parsley* he said:

> ". . . a stigma still attaches to any person convicted of a truly criminal offence, and the more serious or more disgraceful the offence the greater the stigma."

Lord Reid went on to consider the various means by which the law had sought to ameliorate the harshness of the application of strict liability for criminal offences, as by shifting the onus of proof, or by importing concepts of negligence or recklessness.

A standard textbook on criminal law (Smith & Hogan) summarises in the following words the circumstances where the courts tend to interpret a statute as imposing strict liability: 'The greater the degree of social danger, the more likely is the offence to be interpreted as one of strict liability'. The authors cite four examples of areas where strict liability has been invoked 'as a protection for society': inflation, drugs, road safety and pollution. They omit consumer protection, although that is one of the major areas where the doctrine has been applied, and from which they draw examples in other parts of their treatise. These four areas, as the salient examples, together with consumer protection, are worth exploring in a little more detail.

Inflation

In *R v St Margaret's Trust Ltd.* (1958), a finance company was convicted of disposing of a car on HP and taking less than 50 per cent of
the price by way of deposit. This was forbidden by a statutory instru-
ment, made under legislation designed to safeguard the nation's
economy. The finance company had acted entirely innocently,
having been deceived by a car dealer who had falsely stated the pur-
chase price. Nevertheless the finance company was convicted. Mr
Justice Donovan, explaining why the law in such a case made 'an
express and unqualified prohibition of the acts done . . .' said that
Parliament

> ". . . enacted measures which it intended to be absolute prohibitions of
> acts which might increase the risk [of the collapse of the currency] in how-
> ever small a degree. Indeed, that would be the natural expectation. There
> would be little point in enacting that no one should breach the defences
> against a flood, and at the same time excusing anyone who did it inno-
> cently."

Drugs

In relation to dangerous drugs, Parliament and the courts have
steered a somewhat unsteady course in trying to forbid strictly, if
not absolutely, involvement with, as well as use of, dangerous
drugs. In *Warner v Metropolitan Police Commissioner* (1968) the
defendant was held to be guilty of being in unauthorised possession
of a dangerous drug, even though he did not realise that what he had
in his possession in a closed container *was* a drug.

But two years later, in *Sweet v Parsley*, the House of Lords
baulked at convicting a schoolmistress of 'being concerned in the
management of premises used for the purpose of smoking cannabis'
where she was in fact the subtenant of a house in the country, and let
rooms to a variety of people, some of whom smoked cannabis there.
She did not live on the premises, but retained a room for occasional
use, and knew absolutely nothing of the use of cannabis there. The
House of Lords, overruling the court which had convicted her, held
that *mens rea* was required for this offence.

Pollution

There is no doubt, however, that strict liability is still with us. In *Alphacell Ltd v Woodward* in 1972, the House of Lords had little hesitation in upholding the conviction of a company for 'causing . . . polluting matter' to enter a river, contrary to the Rivers (Prevention of Pollution) Act 1951. The company was a paper manufacturer, and drew water from a river in connection with their production processes. The water became polluted by these processes; before being returned to the river, it was purified by being passed through settling tanks. Pumps were installed to prevent any overflow of polluted water from the tanks. This had worked without trouble for some time, and the company maintained a system for the inspection and maintenance of the tanks and the pumps. In spite of this, one day the tanks overflowed and polluted water entered the river. It turned out that this had been due to the pumps becoming blocked by vegetation. There was no evidence that the company had realised this, or could reasonably have done so.

The House of Lords nevertheless held that the company was guilty of the offence under the Act. Lord Salmon said:

> "It is of the utmost public importance that our rivers should not be polluted. The risk of pollution, particularly from the vast and increasing number of riparian industries, is very great. The offences created by the Act of 1951 seem to me to be prototypes of offences which 'are not criminal in any real sense, but are acts which in the public interest are prohibited under a penalty' (*Sherras v De Rutzen*) . . . In the case of a minor pollution such as the present, when the justices find that there is no wrongful intention or negligence on the part of the defendant, a comparatively nominal fine will no doubt be imposed. This may be regarded as a not unfair hazard of carrying on a business which may cause pollution on the banks of a river."

Road traffic

In the branch of the law concerned with road traffic, offences of strict liability abound. There is a large number of offences of a petty character, concerned with every aspect of the bureaucratic requirements that have to be imposed on those who use motor vehicles on roads. Nearly all involve some measure of strict liability.

Driving offences constitute by far the most common involvement of the common man with the criminal law. Relatively few ever feel much shame about being convicted. Speeding, driving with a defective light, and parking offences of varying kinds are familiar examples of crimes which 'are not criminal in any real sense'. Suggestions have been made from time to time for the establishment of traffic courts, with a view to taking significant parts of the road traffic law out of the strictly criminal calendar, but nothing has so far come of these ideas.

Some road traffic offences can be disposed of without criminal proceedings, on payment of a fixed penalty, under section 80 of the Road Traffic Regulation Act 1967. At present, this applies only to offences of a minor character, including those relating to parking, lights, licences and a few others.

In May 1981, the government announced plans to extend greatly the fixed penalty procedure. In future it should apply to speeding and other 'moving traffic' offences, as well as to failure to obey traffic directions (for instance, traffic lights) and offences in relation to construction and use of vehicles. The government working party which recommended these changes estimated that extending the scope of the fixed penalty in this way could relieve the courts of up to 600,000 cases a year, one third of all traffic cases, and save between £3m and £10m a year.

Welcome though these proposals are, they do not change the essential criminal character of the prohibitions in question. They do, however, serve to underline firmly that there are some crimes which do not require to be handled through the strict procedures of the criminal law.

The distinction between real crimes and mere prohibitions which happen to be regulated by the criminal law—there being nothing else to hand to deal with them—is demonstrated by these provisions, and by the plans for their extension.

Road traffic offences which may be dealt with by the fixed penalty procedure are, by definition, the very ones which ought to cease to be criminal offences at all, and be transferred to a middle system of law, and so made subject to civil penalties only.

Consumer law

In consumer law, there are many criminal offences of strict liability, where no *mens rea* need be proved. The most familiar are under the Weights and Measures Act 1963, the Food and Drugs Act 1955, the Trade Descriptions Act 1968, the Consumer Credit Act 1974 and the Consumer Safety Act 1978.

An early case upholding the principle of strict liability under the criminal law in relation to consumer affairs was *Hobbs v Winchester Corporation* (1910), concerning a butcher charged with selling unsound meat. He was held to be liable, even though he was not aware that the meat was unsound, and could not have discovered by any examination he could reasonably be expected to have made that it was unsound. Lord Justice Kennedy explained the rationale for imposing strict liability in these words:

> "The clear object, the important object [of the statute] . . . is, as far as possible, to protect the buyer of that which, in the opinion at all events of most people, is a necessity of human life, from buying and consuming meat that is unwholesome and unfit for the food of man; and I should say that the natural inference from the statute and its object is that the peril to the butcher from innocently selling unsound meat is deemed by the legislature to be much less than the peril to the public which would follow from the necessity in each case of proving a *mens rea* . . . I think that the policy of the Act is this: that if a man chooses for profit to engage in a business which involves the offering for sale of that which may be deadly or injurious to health, he must take that risk, and that it is not a sufficient defence for any one who chooses to embark on such a business to say 'I could not have discovered the disease unless I had an analyst on the premises'."

The principle has been greatly extended in the last 70 years, and now covers not only matters affecting the health and safety of consumers, but also their economic interests; bargain offers and consumer credit are examples. The control of bargain offers, introduced in 1979 under the Prices Act 1974, makes it a criminal offence for a shopkeeper to claim—even if it is true—that his price for a bed, or a radio or a television set, or similar item, is less by a stated amount than the price recommended for it by its manufacturer.

In legislation imposing strict liability in the consumer area, a defence is usually available to a trader who can prove (and the burden of proof is on him) that the offence was caused by some thing beyond his control, such as the act or default of someone else, and that he took all reasonable precautions and exercised all due diligence to prevent committing the offence himself. This mitigates to a

considerable extent the harshness of the application of strict liability
where a defendant is really blameless.

In *Tesco v Nattrass* in 1971, the House of Lords decided that the
'someone else' whose act or default would excuse what would otherwise be an infringement of the Trade Descriptions Act 1968 could
include the defendant's own shop manager, in the case of a large
supermarket chain. As a result, strict liability can hardly be said to
apply to big companies under this legislation, provided they can
show that at the top a system of compliance with the legislation is
properly organised. 'Due diligence' is required at that level only,
and employees who were at fault at the managerial or shop level are
not identified with the company. This somewhat surprising decision—surely not what was intended by Parliament—can only be
explained in terms of the House of Lords' determination to ease the
impact of an offence of strict liability on the commercial community. Lord Morris said '. . . it is important to remember that it is the
criminal liability of the company itself that is being considered. In
general criminal liability only results from personal fault. We do not
punish people in criminal courts for the misdeeds of others.'

The case is a good example of the reluctance of the courts to apply
strict liability, when it comes to it. Lord Diplock's remarks about
the underlying philosophy of strict liability in its application to consumer protection are worth quoting at some length. He said:

> "Consumer protection, which is the purpose of statutes of this kind, is
> achieved only if the occurrence of the prohibited acts or omissions is pre-
> vented. It is the deterrent effect of penal provisions which protects the
> consumer from the loss he would sustain if the offence were committed.
> If it is committed he does not receive the amount of any fine. As a taxpayer
> he will bear part of the expense of maintaining a convicted offender in
> prison. The loss to the consumer is the same whether the acts or omissions
> which result in his being given inaccurate or inadequate information are
> intended to mislead him, or are due to carelessness or inadvertence. So is
> the corresponding gain to the other party to the business transaction with
> the consumer in the course of which those acts or omissions occur.
> Where, in the way that business is now conducted, they are likely to be acts
> or omissions of employees of that party and subject to his orders, the most
> effective method of deterrence is to place on the employer the responsibil-
> ity of doing everything which lies within his power to prevent his
> employees from doing anything which will result in the commission of an
> offence.
>   This, I apprehend, is the rational and moral justification for creating in
> the field of consumer protection, as also in the field of public health and
> safety, offences of 'strict liability' for which an employer or principal, in
> the course of whose business the offences were committed, is criminally
> liable, notwithstanding that they are due to acts or omissions of his ser-

vants or agents which were done without his knowledge or consent or even were contrary to his orders. But this rational and moral justification does not extend to penalising an employer or principal who has done everything that he can reasonably be expected to do by supervision or inspection, by improvement of his business methods or by exhorting those whom he may be expected to control or influence, to prevent the commission of the offence . . ."

As with road traffic law, the feeling is widespread that a conviction for an offence under consumer protection laws is 'not criminal in any real sense'. It is not likely that a trader will be unable to hold up his head in his local chamber of commerce if it becomes known that he had been 'done' under the Trade Descriptions Act, or that, by inadvertance or bad luck, a nail was found in one of his loaves of bread, giving rise to a conviction under the Food and Drugs Act 1955.

Professor Glanville Williams, one of today's leading jurists, deals with the subject of strict liability in his *Textbook of Criminal Law* (1978), under the general heading of 'Regulatory Offences'.

He cites the case of *Parker v Alder* (1899) as an example of strict liability in an area or law concerned with consumer protection. In that case, a farmer was convicted of selling milk which was not of the nature, substance and quality demanded, contrary to what is now the Food and Drugs Act. An unknown person had added water to milk churns, without any fault on the part of the farmer. Professor Williams comments:

"It is, in a way, only a minor evil that a farmer should be made to pay a fine of a few pounds, which he can well afford, for the adulteration of milk, even though he could not help it. However, if this is an evil it has the characteristic of being an unnecessary one, since there is generally no compelling need to have strict liability in crime. Careless breaches of regulatory offences abound, and prosecutions for these are usually sufficient to be a standing warning to people to obey the law. Little purpose is served by adding to the large numbers of truly guilty defendants the small number of persons who are morally innocent. The social argument is all the other way. For whereas natural evils can often be accepted as part of the price of living, a man-made evil may be strongly and even bitterly resented because it is felt to be unjust.

A fine imposed upon a business concern irrespective of fault is not so much an affront as is a fine imposed upon an individual. But even if the defendant is a trading concern, the result of a rule disregarding fault may be that business men come to regard fines as part of their overhead costs, as unavoidable and unpredictable as the English weather."

This sentiment is echoed by Mr Gordon Borrie, the Director General of Fair Trading, in an important speech made in March

1980 to the Association of Law Teachers. Dealing with the role of the criminal law in consumer affairs, he asked:

> "What are the weaknesses or disadvantages of the criminal law? One is that at least with some traders, convictions are treated as tiresome pinpricks, minor inconveniences that are shrugged off and the fines put down as a business expense."

Professor Williams continued with this dire warning:

> "The attitude of indifference which is thus engendered towards the criminal process through inflation of the law may well spread to other offences, where an element of fault is present. Often it is cheaper to run the risk of an occasional small fine than to make the alterations in business arrangements necessary to avoid it. If the trader becomes habituated to the atmosphere of the criminal court, and is taught to regard the criminal process as something that has no connection with responsibility and fault, he may adopt a cynical and self-interested attitude on many of the questions to which legal regulations are directed. The ultimate result may actually be a decrease in the preventive effect of the law."

Here then is important support for the proposition that the huge expansion in regulatory law has debased the coinage of the criminal law. One way of restoring to the criminal law and its administration some of the awe for which it was once famous is to hive off those parts which are not 'criminal in any real sense', and place them in a new middle system.

Professor Williams then discusses what motivates Parliament in making strict liability apply to certain offences. He says:

> "It is sometimes said that strict liability is imposed where the offence is the result of modern legislative policy and not of traditional morality, or in other words where it is a matter of *malum prohibitum* rather than *malum in se*. This view was expressed, for example, by Lord Reid (in *Sweet v Parsley*). *Mala prohibita* are sometimes called 'quasi-criminal offences'— offences that are regarded as 'not criminal in any real sense, but acts which in the public interest are prohibited under penalty'. They are also called 'public welfare offences' or 'regulatory offences'. To use these expressions is easier than to say exactly what they mean. The so-called quasi-criminal offences are followed by the same procedure for prosecution and kinds of punishment as other offences. All offences are, in a sense, public welfare offences, and all result from legal regulation.
>
> Perhaps the argument is that a person's reputation is not lowered because he is found guilty of a technical offence, and in such a case people are not interested to know whether he committed the offence knowingly or not. One can indeed make a broad distinction between technical offences and particularly disgraceful acts, but it is a matter of degree. If the principle is that strict liability applies only to technical offences, the courts have an idiosyncratic idea of what constitutes such an offence."

Professor Williams later turns to the question of prosecution policy in relation to offences of strict liability.

". . . where offences are very numerous, a requirement that the prosecutor should prove fault may impose a burden upon the resources of law-enforcement out of proportion to the end to be achieved. Such a requirement might mean that the police, or inspectors of health and safety at work, or traffic examiners, or trading standards officers, should possess a larger investigative staff than they do at present. But this argument, again, does not carry complete conviction. For one thing, the police and government inspectors do not come down like a wolf on the fold. They generally consider the question of fault when deciding whether to prosecute, and they are adjured to do this by the courts. In *Smedleys Ltd v Breed,* where canners were convicted because of the presence of a caterpillar in a tin of peas, Viscount Dilhorne said:

'In this case when full information was given by the appellants before the information was laid, I am, I must confess, entirely at a loss to see on what grounds it could have been thought that a prosecution was desirable to protect the general interest of consumers.

The exercise by food and drugs authorities of discretion in the institution of criminal proceedings and the omission to do so where they consider that a prosecution will serve no useful purpose is no more the exercise of a dispensing power than the omission of the law officers, the Director of Public Prosecutions and the police to prosecute for an offence. I have never heard it suggested that the failure of the police to prosecute for every traffic offence which comes to their notice is an exercise by them of a dispensing power'."

Professor Williams comments:

"Certainly it is desirable, as things are, that prosecutors should exercise a discretion. But the result is that the real trial takes place in the prosecutor's office, or (in the case of road traffic offences) in the police station, without any of the safeguards of a proper trial, and perhaps without the suspect even being fully heard. If the prosecutor decides to go forward, the courts simply rubber-stamp his decision and convict."

At the end of this passage Professor Williams proclaims:

"Strict liability is apt to create a burning sense of grievance and a loss of confidence in the administration of the law."

Towards an answer

The result of the growth of crimes of strict liability is that people convicted of them and members of the public who hear of them, no longer regard them as 'criminal in any real sense'.

Crimes which are not crimes in any real sense have no business being crimes at all. The answer is to transform their character, so that they continue to be forbidden and remain unlawful, but that they cease to be crimes. Sanctions—in the form of civil penalties—could be introduced for such transgressions. If they were, Parliament, the courts, enforcement agencies, the public, to say nothing of the transgressors themselves, would have an altogether more appropriate attitude to the law.

Many of the problems that arise from enacting offences of strict liability would be eased by adopting civil penalties as the sanction. One of the deficiencies of the present system is the 'all or nothing at all' approach. A trader who has committed a technical infringement (the canners in the case concerning the caterpillar in the tin of peas, for instance) either gets prosecuted, convicted and fined, with all the rigmarole of the criminal law, or he gets away with it completely. In marginal cases, the prosecuting authority decides, behind closed doors, and according to criteria which are neither publicly accounted for, nor uniform throughout the land, whether or not to prosecute. In fairness to him, as well as to the trader, there ought to be a third option. This is what the middle system of law would provide.

Those at present prosecuted and convicted for technical offences would cease to feel a sense of grievance or outrage at being branded criminals for acts which were not 'criminal in any real sense'. Most, however, recognise the need for a law on the subject, and that this necessarily entails some sanction. The payment of a civil penalty for such infringements would generally feel quite different from the payment of a fine, although the cost may be the same.

It is legitimate to speculate that in many cases the cost might well be greater when a civil penalty were awarded. Under the present system, magistrates who convict traders and motorists of purely technical offences sometimes indicate their sympathy with the defendants before them by imposing small and even nominal fines for such offences. The very fact of being convicted of a crime is sometimes considered enough punishment—perhaps disproportionate to the fault or blame that may have been involved—so that the actual fine is sometimes nominal. Under the new system, the court may well feel much more at ease in awarding a civil penalty that really hurts, once the obloquy of a criminal conviction is removed from the transgression. So far as prosecution policy is concerned, enforcement agencies may well feel more relaxed about proceeding with a claim for an infringement of the law, when the outcome will be the award of a civil penalty.

The criminal law will always be there to deal with cases which *are* 'criminal in any real sense': for matters involving fraud, for instance, in the area of consumer affairs. The introduction of a middle system of law, with civil penalties as the sanction, would provide nothing more than an additional option to enforcing agencies. They could still prosecute for a crime, where they were dealing with crooks, and could prove it. One of the disadvantages of the present system is that the distinction between real crooks and technical offenders is not clear.

Where *mens rea* could not be proved, the prosecutor would be free to seek a civil penalty, and in many cases defendants would be pleased not to be prosecuted, and to accept without demur that the matter should be disposed of by payment of a civil penalty. Honour would thus be satisfied all round, without resentment, and with a considerable saving to public funds.

It would no doubt take some years—perhaps decades—before the concept of a new system of law really took hold in our legal system, and the legal professions, the judiciary, the magistracy, the enforcement agencies and the public fully accepted the role of the new system in the administration of justice. But once it had, much good would come of it.

In the United States

In the United States, the National Commission on Reform of Federal Criminal Laws published in 1970 a 'Proposed New Federal Criminal Code'. In the Working Papers supporting this, the Commission dealt with what it termed 'regulatory offences', and suggested that the legislature should consider including a declaration of policy regarding the use of such regulatory laws.

This declaration of policy is worth quoting; it applies equally to the situation in the UK, and aptly summarises the dilemma of legislatures throughout the common law world in seeking to control behaviour beyond the realm of 'real' crime. It is as follows:

> "Declaration of Policy. The great increase of statutory and administrative regulation commanding affirmative acts or forbidding behaviour not condemned by generally recognised ethical standards emphasises the need for discrimination in the use of the criminal law to enforce such regulation. Use of penal sanctions to enforce regulation involves substantial risk that a person may be subjected to conviction, disgrace, and punishment although he did not know that his conduct was wrongful. When penal sanctions are employed for regulatory offences, considerations with respect to fair treatment of human beings, as well as the substantive aims of the regulatory statute, must enter into legislative, judicial and administrative decisions with regard to sanctions. It is the policy of the United States to prefer nonpenal sanctions over penal sanctions to secure compliance with regulatory law unless violation of regulation manifests disregard for the welfare of others or of the authority of government . . ."

Elsewhere in the report, the following comment is made, also applicable to the situation in the UK:

> "Criminal law has always differentiated between two kinds of punishable behaviour. On the one hand, homicide, rape, robbery and the other common law crimes are universally recognised outrages and threats to common security. Common morality forbids such behaviour, and there is little possibility of innocent transgression. Commission of offences of this sort evidences a serious disregard for the rights of other individuals, and identifies the offender as dangerous because of his lack of inhibitions and distorted system of values. Traditionally, offences of this first type have been designated 'mala in se', that is, 'evil in themselves', in contrast with the other category of offences 'malum prohibitum', that is, 'bad because forbidden'.
>
> The regulatory statutes . . . belong in the 'malum prohibitum' class. The behaviour is not immediately recognisable as evil or dangerous, and does not necessarily identify the actor as immoral. In a complex modern society, there are hundreds of thousands of legal commands and prohibitions, violation of which may incur criminal liability. The motor vehicle

laws offer the best examples: driving over the speed limit or without a license, failure to carry a registration card or a safety inspection certificate, parking in a prohibited zone, passing a stopped school bus, and a host of others. The conduct of business is often minutely controlled by statute and by rules and orders issued by administrative agencies. . . . Included are regulations protecting the safety and comfort of passengers by ship, airplane, rail and motor carriers; food and drug controls; animal inspection and quarantine; prohibitions of rate discrimination, deceptive advertising, and other unfair business practices; license and inspection requirements for various businesses; regulation of packaging and labelling; compulsory maintenance of records and filing of reports.

. . . It is characteristic of regulatory controls that they are prophylactic in purpose; that the standards of behaviour are detailed, specific, and subject to change and development . . .

The prophylactic purpose means that the rules are designed to *prevent* harms from occurring, rather than to punish the perpetrators of actual harms . . . Two more identifying characteristics of 'regulatory' offences may be noted. . . . It will often be found that regulations apply to particular groups, e.g. distillers, drug manufacturers, public officials, operators of specified public service facilities, rather than to the general public; and that nonpenal sanctions are more effective than penal sanctions for this kind of misbehaviour. License suspension, forfeiture of illegal goods, *civil penalties* (emphasis added), dismissal from employment—these may be more drastic and more appropriate than prosecution."

The report of the US National Commission on Reform of the Federal Criminal Code then goes on to consider the place in the proposed code of various degrees of culpability.

"The punishment . . . provided may be merely a civil penalty . . . That would be enough to show Congress' intention to penalize violations."

The report then suggests that *wilful* violations should be regarded as misdemeanours, that is, crimes in the normal sense. It says:

"Civil penalties have a useful place in law enforcement, but it does not make sense to treat continuing purposeful defiance of regulatory authority as a purely civil matter."

In the United States, civil penalties are often used as sanctions for regulatory laws. Two examples from the consumer field illustrate this.

Unfair and deceptive acts and practices

The Federal Trade Commission is the main government agency involved in consumer protection at federal level. The original Federal Trade Commission Act gave the FTC broad authority to regulate 'unfair or deceptive acts or practices'. Until 1975 the only way the FTC could enforce these powers was by the use of 'cease and desist' orders, a civil procedure. These were found to be cumbersome and ineffective in practice.

In that year the Magnuson-Moss Warranty-Federal Trade Commission Improvement Act was passed. This has considerably improved the FTC's enforcement powers. The actual language of the Act demonstrates how, in a consumer context, a provision imposing a civil penalty might read in a UK context. Leaving out parts of the wording which are not strictly relevant, the section of the 1975 Act reads:

> "The Commission may commence a civil action to recover a civil penalty . . . against any . . . corporation which violates any rule under this Act respecting unfair or deceptive acts or practices . . . with actual knowledge or knowledge fairly implied . . . that such act is unfair or deceptive and is prohibited by such rule. In such action, such . . . corporation shall be liable for a civil penalty of not more than $10,000 for each violation."

The section later provides that in the event of continuing violation

> "each day of continuance of such failure shall be treated as a separate violation . . ."

Consumer safety

Another example in the United States is to be found in the Consumer Product Safety Act. This was passed in 1972 and set up the Consumer Product Safety Commission. The Act enables federal consumer safety standards to be imposed, and products which are found to be hazardous can be banned.

Section 19 of the Act states that:

> "It shall be unlawful for any person to—
> manufacture for sale, offer for sale . . . any consumer product which has been declared a banned hazardous product by a rule under this Act . . ."

Section 20 states:

> "Any person who knowingly violates section 19 of this Act shall be subject to a civil penalty not to exceed $2,000 for each such violation . . . A violation of section 19 . . . shall constitute a separate offense with respect to each consumer product involved except that the maximum civil penalty shall not exceed $500,000 for any related series of violations . . ."

Section 20 goes on to provide that 'any civil penalty under this section may be compromised by the Commission', that is, can be disposed of without taking proceedings, if agreement between the Commission and the business concerned can be reached. The section ends by stating that 'knowingly' in the first sentence means

> "the having of actual knowledge, or the presumed having of knowledge deemed to be possessed by a reasonable man who acts in the circumstances, including knowledge obtainable upon the exercise of due care to ascertain the truth of representations".

The Consumer Product Safety Act then goes on to make provision for criminal penalties. Section 21 says:

> "Any person who knowingly and willfully violates section 19 of this Act after having received notice of noncompliance from the Commission shall be fined not more than $50,000 or be imprisoned not more than one year, or both".

This could point the way for a 'two tier' system of sanctions in legislation in the UK: a civil penalty to be exacted for relatively minor infringements, a criminal penalty for the more serious ones.

Civil law

The role of the civil law traditionally was to regulate private relationships between individuals, by conferring rights on individuals, and imposing obligations in the dealings of one citizen with another and with authorities. The rights of citizens and their enforcement are a matter for the civil courts, and it is usually up to the individual citizen to obtain his rights, if they are denied him, by taking proceedings in the civil court. In this way he can obtain payment of his debts, compensation for wrongs done to him and injunctions to forbid future infringements of his rights. This is still the main function of the civil law.

In recent times, however, the civil law has been utilised by Parliament to fulfil an additional social purpose. In some instances, Parliament determines that certain behaviour should be controlled by law, but appears to recoil from the notion of prohibiting that behaviour through the criminal law. Instead, it declares behaviour to be unlawful, and then provides means through the civil law to enforce compliance. Examples of this are race and sex discrimination, restrictive practices and, in some aspects, industrial relations.

Race relations

The Race Relations Act 1976 is a notable example of society determining to deal with a social evil—racial discrimination—and finding that the existing legal structures and procedures do not really present an appropriate means of regulating the behaviour sought to be brought within the law.

Controlling race relations by law was politically and socially controversial; many people believed that it was not only impossible but inappropriate. They argued that the law should not be involved with what is, in essence, the attitudes of one group in society about another group, and that race relations ought to be handled, not by law, but by persuasion and example.

It was never seriously suggested that racial discrimination as such should be a criminal offence. The only aspect of the law about race relations which is within the criminal law is incitement to racial hatred. Section 70 of the Race Relations Act 1976 introduced an addition of the Public Order Act 1936 by enacting that

"A person commits an offence if—
(a) he publishes or distributes written matter which is threatening, abusive or insulting; or
(b) he uses in any public place or at any public meeting words which are threatening, abusive or insulting,
in a case where having regard to all the circumstances, hatred is likely to be stirred up against any racial group in Great Britain by the matter or words in question".

Virtually all the rest of the Race Relations Act is part of the civil law. Discrimination is defined as taking place when a person on racial grounds—those of colour, race, nationality or ethnic or national origins—treats another person less favourably than he treats or would treat other persons. Section 4 declares

"It is unlawful for a person, in relation to employment by him at an establishment in Great Britain, to discriminate against another . . ."

The Act continues in similar vein, declaring a whole series of acts 'unlawful':

"It is unlawful for an employment agency to discriminate against a person" (section 14);
"It is unlawful, in relation to an educational establishment . . . to discriminate against a person" (section 17);
"It is unlawful for any person concerned with the provision (for payment or not) of goods, facilities or services to the public or a section of the public to discriminate against a person who seeks to obtain or use those goods, facilities or services . . ." (section 20).

What, then, are the consequences of these acts being declared unlawful? For discrimination in relation to employment, section 54 provides that a person can bring a claim in the appropriate industrial tribunal, where his rights in the matter can be declared, and he can be awarded compensation.

Other kinds of discrimination are dealt with by section 57. A person who claims to have been discriminated against can bring a claim in the county court "in like manner as any other claim in tort . . .' This seems to indicate that it was the draftsman's intention that racial discrimination should be a tort.

Damages are recoverable for breach. Subsection (4) declares 'for the avoidance of doubt' that 'damages in respect of an unlawful act of discrimination may include compensation for injury to feelings whether or not they include compensation under any other head'.

In practice, not many people bring civil proceedings for damages for unlawful discrimination. Perhaps Parliament expected this, for in reality enforcement of the Act is substantially in the hands of the Commission for Racial Equality. Section 58 empowers the Commission to issue a non-discrimination notice, a document requiring the person alleged to be in breach of the requirements of the Act 'not to commit any such acts", that is any unlawful discriminatory act. Before serving a non-discrimination notice, the Commission has to give notice of an intention to do so, stating the grounds, and offer an opportunity of representations to be made about the matter. The person who receives a non-discrimination notice can appeal to the industrial tribunal or the county court.

There is no sanction in the Act for failure to comply with a single non-discrimination notice. But once a notice has been served, and becomes final and it appears to the Commission that, unless restrained, the person concerned 'is likely to do one or more acts' of discrimination, the Commission can apply to the county court for an injunction. An injunction is the ultimate sanction for persistent unlawful acts of discrimination, carrying with it the threat of imprisonment for contempt of court if it is not complied with.

Sex discrimination

The Sex Discrimination Act 1975 is similar in many respects to the Race Relations Act, but there are no criminal provisions.

Acts of sex discrimination in employment, education, housing and the provision of goods, facilities and services are declared to be 'unlawful'.

As with racial discrimination, the industrial tribunal deals with complaints of unlawful discrimination affecting employment, and the tribunal has the power to award compensation, where unlawful discrimination is proved. Other kinds of discrimination are dealt with in the county court. Claims 'may be made the subject of civil proceedings in like manner as any other claim in tort . . .'

But the main effective enforcement lies in the hands of the enforcement agency, in this case the Equal Opportunities Commission. Again, a non-discrimination notice can be issued by the Commission requiring the unlawful discrimination to cease, and an appeal against such a notice can be made to the industrial tribunal or to the county court. In the case of persistent discrimination, the Commission may apply to a county court for an injunction (section

71) restraining a person from continuing to commit unlawful acts of discrimination. Under section 75, the Commission may provide assistance to anyone in connection with the bringing of proceedings for unlawful discrimination under the Act.

In the newly developed law of discrimination, therefore, we find Parliament stopping short of making discrimination an offence, but providing for a public body to be able, through a rather cumbersome procedure invoking the civil law and its sanctions, to stop future breaches of the law that are persistent. There is no provision in either Act for the payment of a penalty for past acts of discrimination, only for the award of compensation to victims who bring a claim. Perhaps it did not occur to anyone that it would have been possible to have declared discrimination unlawful without making it a criminal offence, and to have provided a sanction in the form of a civil penalty for breach.

Fair Trading Act 1973

Another example of the way that Parliament has used the civil law to control antisocial behaviour is found in Part III of the Fair Trading Act 1973. The aim of this part of the Act is to provide a means of stopping traders from persistently breaking the law. For some crooked or doubtful traders, being prosecuted and fined for breach of, say, the Trade Descriptions Act 1968 or the Food and Drugs Act 1955 was no deterrent against breaking the law in the future. Often the fines were not enough to make significant inroads into the money being made by operating outside the law—the fines were regarded as part of the expenses of running the business. So Part III of the 1973 Act provides a procedure for invoking the civil law to come to the aid of the criminal law. The procedure can also be used for persistent breaches of the civil law, for example, where a shop regularly refuses to give buyers their money back for defective goods.

Section 34 enables the Director General of Fair Trading to seek assurances from traders who have engaged in a course of conduct which is detrimental to the interests of consumers, and is unfair to them. The section specifies what is to be regarded as unfair, namely, conduct which consists 'of contraventions . . . of enactments which impose duties, prohibitions or restrictions enforceable by criminal proceedings . . .' as well as 'things done, or omitted to be done, . . . in breach of contract or in breach of a duty . . . enforceable by civil proceedings . . .'.

If the Director fails to get an assurance from the trader that he will refrain in future from the offending course of conduct, or if such an assurance is given and broken, the Director 'may bring proceedings against him before the Restrictive Practices Court'. Unless the trader then provides the appropriate undertaking, the court can make an order directing the trader 'to refrain from continuing that course of conduct'. By section 41, the Director can in certain cases bring proceedings in the county court instead.

If the trader fails to comply with an order of the court made under Part III of the Fair Trading Act, he is guilty of contempt of court, and can be sent to prison for this.

This procedure has been used with considerable success. A total of 182 Part III assurances were given in the first six years that the provisions were in operation. As a rule, the Director General of Fair Trading has not had to resort to legal proceedings.

These provisions are an attempt by Parliament to deal with the middle ground by using the civil law to enforce consistent compliance with both the civil and the criminal law. They provide a useful beginning along the road towards a middle system of law.

Other aspects

There are other areas of the law where using civil penalties as the sanction could be contemplated. Employment law is one. It could be, for example, that at least some aspects of the law of picketing are appropriate for regulation by civil penalties.

Education is another example. When education for all became an important principle of public policy, it had to be made compulsory for all, and in order to make education compulsory, it had to be made a criminal offence for a parent to allow a child to be absent from school without an excuse. It would, however, have been sufficient to have enunciated the principle of compulsory education and to have given this principle the force of law by making failure to provide education subject to the sanction of a civil penalty.

Civil penalties are the most appropriate sanction to use when Parliament wishes to enshrine in a statute a universal principle for which compliance is likely to be general, and enforcement comparatively unimportant. Education, sex and race equality, privacy, and conservation questions are examples of such principles. It is a way by which a general principle of public policy can be declared and given the force of law, without involving criminal liability.

Civil penalties under existing UK law

The failure on the part of the UK legislature to provide civil penalties as a general sanction for the contravention of regulatory laws is surprising when one remembers the shining example emanating from that very legislature itself.

Tax law

Civil penalties are the main sanction used by UK fiscal legislation to procure adherence by the population to the tax laws. There is perhaps no other branch of the law which so consistently and powerfully impinges on the lives of so many people, mainly hitting them in their pockets. It is surprising, therefore, that the legal sanctions for the enforcement of these laws have not been applied in other branches of the law which fall in the middle ground of social behaviour.

The Taxes Management Act 1970 (consolidating provisions which date back to the 1840's) contains the main framework for the operation of our tax laws and provides the machinery for its collection and the sanction for its implementation.

Section 93 of the 1970 Act says:

> "If any person has been required by a notice . . . to deliver any return, and he fails to comply with the notice he shall be liable . . . to a penalty not exceeding . . . £50, and if the failure continues after it has been declared by the court . . . to a further penalty not exceeding £10 for each day on which the failure so continues."

Section 95 deals with incorrect returns or accounts:

> "Where a person fraudulently or negligently delivers any incorrect return . . . or makes any incorrect . . . statement or declaration in connection with any claim for any allowance, deduction or relief in respect of income tax or capital gains tax, or submits to an inspector . . . any incorrect accounts in connection with the ascertainment of his liability to income tax or capital gains tax, he shall be liable to a penalty . . ."

The section then sets out how the penalty is to be calculated: it is a sum not exceeding the aggregate of £50 and the amount of tax he would have avoided paying had he got away with it. In the case of fraud, the penalty can be £50 plus *twice* the amount of tax that would have been avoided.

Criminal proceedings can be brought in respect of incorrect returns and accounts sent to the tax man, where an intent to defraud can be proved. Often criminal proceedings are brought for the common law offence of practising a fraud on the public revenue.

But the number of prosecutions brought by the Inland Revenue is relatively insignificant. For the year 1978/79 a mere 192 people were prosecuted in criminal proceedings brought by the Inland Revenue, of whom 8 were acquitted. In the previous year it was even fewer. Only 156 were prosecuted, of whom 8 were acquitted.

Compare those figures with the numbers dealt with under the penalty provisions of the tax legislation. For the year ended 31 October 1979, a total of 21,376 charges were raised against defaulting taxpayers involving negligence, wilful default or fraud. These taxpayers paid a total of over £11m by way of penalties. For the previous year, 18,521 charges were made and over £9m paid by way of penalties.

In each of those years, therefore, over 99 per cent of the cases dealt with by the Inland Revenue where something was amiss were disposed of by way of civil penalties, leaving less than one per cent dealt with by criminal proceedings. Overwhelmingly, the Revenue relies on the penalty provisions of the tax laws as the effective sanction for their enforcement.

Where taxpayers are fraudulent in seeking to evade tax and the tax inspector catches up with them, they are invited to come clean and to make a full confession of their 'guilt'. It is represented to them that if they do so, their wrongdoing might be dealt with by a civil penalty, rather than by criminal proceedings. They are also told that the making of a full confession could well play a part in the determination of the amount of the penalty they may have to pay. Official policy about this has been carefully laid down, and the basis of present practice remains as stated in the House of Commons in 1944:

> ". . . the Commissioners (of Inland Revenue) have a general power under which they can accept pecuniary settlements instead of instituting criminal proceedings in respect of fraud or wilful default alleged to have been committed by a taxpayer. They can, however, give no undertaking to a taxpayer in any such case that they will accept such a settlement and refrain from instituting criminal proceedings even if the case is one in which the taxpayer has made full confession and has given full facilities for investigation of the facts. They reserve to themselves complete discretion in all cases as to the course which they will pursue, but it is their practice to be influenced by the fact that the taxpayer has made a full confession and has given full facilities for investigation into his affairs and for examination of

such books, papers, documents or information as the Commissioners may consider necessary".

Thus, where fraud on the part of a taxpayer comes to light, the Revenue has full discretion whether to proceed under the criminal system or under the middle system. This works pretty well in practice, and is the model for the expansion of the middle system into other areas requiring control by law.

Electricity

Another interesting example of the use of civil penalties in our legal system is to be found in the Electric Lighting (Clauses) Act 1899. This Act still provides much of the legal framework for the generation and supply of electricity in this country. It was enacted on the assumption that electricity would be provided by individual statutory undertakers, long before the electricity industry was nationalised. It sets out the obligations which by law are imposed on the supplier and consumer of electricity. The sanctions for compliance with the code regarding electricity supply are set out in the schedule to the 1899 Act. In most cases this sanction is a civil penalty.

Paragraph 30 of the schedule to the 1899 Act, under the heading 'Penalty for failure to supply' says:

"(1) Whenever the Undertakers make default in supplying energy to any owner or occupier of premises to whom they may be and are required to supply energy under [this schedule], they shall be liable in respect of each default to a penalty not exceeding forty shillings for each day on which the default occurs.

(2) Where . . . the Undertakers make default in supplying energy to the public lamps to which they may be and are required to supply energy under [this schedule], the Undertakers shall be liable in respect of each default to a penalty not exceeding forty shillings for each lamp, and for each day on which the default occurs.

(3) Whenever the Undertakers make default in supplying energy in accordance with the terms of the [Electricity regulations] they shall be liable to such penalties as are prescribed by the regulations in that behalf.

(4) Provided that the penalties to be inflicted on the Undertakers under this section shall in no case exceed in the aggregate in respect of any defaults not being wilful defaults on the part of the Undertakers the sum of fifty pounds for any one day, and provided also that in no case shall any penalty be inflicted in respect of any default if the court are of opinion that the default was caused by inevitable accident or force majeure or was of so

slight or unimportant a character as not materially to affect the value of the supply."

Corresponding penalties are imposed on consumers in this legislation (which was originally intended to apply to gas as well) for the fraudulent use of energy, for wilfully damaging meters and several similar matters. For example:

"38. Every person who wilfully, fraudulently, or by culpable negligence injures or suffers to be injured any . . . meter . . . belonging to the Undertakers . . . shall . . . for every such offence forfeit and pay to the Undertakers a sum not exceeding five pounds . . ."

Paragraph 76 of the schedule to the 1899 Act says:

"76. All penalties, fees, expenses, and other moneys recoverable under [this schedule], or under the [Electricity regulations], the recovery of which is not otherwise specially provided for, may be recovered summarily in manner provided by the Summary Jurisdiction Acts."

This now means recoverable under section 50 of the Magistrates Courts Act 1952:

"50. **Money recoverable summarily as civil debt**
(1) A magistrates' court shall have power to make an order on complaint for the payment of any money recoverable summarily as a civil debt.
　　(2) Any sum payment of which may be ordered by a magistrates' court shall be recoverable summarily as a civil debt . . ."

Here, then, is an existing precedent for civil penalties under our legal system, recoverable in proceedings to be brought in the courts, as distinct from special tribunals constituted for the purpose, as with tax.

Codes of practice

The Director General of Fair Trading has a duty under section 124 (3) of the Fair Trading Act 1973 to encourage trade associations to prepare and operate codes of practice for guidance in safeguarding the interests of consumers. By 1980 there were 19 codes of practice which had been negotiated with the support of the OFT, and although views differ about them, and some codes have had a greater impact than others, on the whole they have been a considerable success. So much so, indeed, that from time to time consideration is given to how they might be extended, and how their effectiveness might be increased.

Mr Gordon Borrie, the Director General of Fair Trading, addressing the Association of Law Teachers in March 1980, said:

> "Codes of practice, however, have particular weaknesses and they are implicit in the very nature of self-regulatory codes negotiated with trade associations—difficulty of enforcement and non-applicability to those traders who are not members of the relevant association. Enforcement depends on the discipline of the trade association itself . . .
>
> The Retail Consortium's answer to these weaknesses of the present self-regulatory codes is to say that they should constitute requirements that *all* traders must follow, and by an extension of Part III of the Fair Trading Act the DGFT should be enabled to seek assurances and take to court any traders who break the codes. Presumably the existing codes would have to be re-negotiated between the OFT and the associations, because they were all originally negotiated on the basis that they were in no way enforceable in the courts".

The Director General then referred to the proposals put forward in 1979 by the Government Working Party on the self-regulatory system of advertising controls. He said:

> "What the government working party recommends has a number of similarities to the Retail Consortium's proposals for codes of practice generally, namely that a general duty should be created by statute that no one should publish an advertisement likely to deceive or mislead with regard to any material fact, and the DGFT should be empowered to seek from the courts an order to prevent the publication of a particular advertisement when in his view publication of it would constitute a breach of the general duty. Failure to obey such an order would be a contempt of court. The idea of such a novel injunctive procedure would be to provide practical reinforcement to the machinery of the ASA [Advertising Standards Authority] where this had been frustrated or was unlikely to be effective . . ."

These ideas about enhancing the role of codes of practice demonstrate that the strict division between the criminal and civil law leaves a dilemma for the legislature, and for those who propose reform. It is understandable that they should baulk at the idea of making non-compliance with a code of practice a criminal offence. Indeed to do so would be impossible, for by so doing a code would cease to be one, but would become part of the criminal law. Neither would it be appropriate to provide sanctions under the civil law, as suggested by the Retail Consortium and the Government Working Party on Advertising. As with the law on discrimination, this could only operate after the event, and prevent through court action future infringements of the law. Past infringements would go scot free.

There are plenty of other codes of practice operating within our social system. Ways are currently being sought to give them 'teeth', meaning presumably giving them in some way the force of law. In at least one notable example, a code *has* been given the force of law. This is in the Weights and Measures Act 1979, which introduced the concept of the average weight system into our law. The duty to pack goods according to the average system is specified in general in section 1, and in detail in the regulations made under that section. Section 2 says: 'A person who fails to perform a duty imposed on him by the preceding section shall be guilty of an offence', with a maximum fine of £1000 as the possible consequence. Those duties include compliance with the provisions of the Packers' Code.

Section 1 (8) says:

> ". . . regulations may provide . . . for questions as to the suitability of equipment . . . to be determined . . . by reference to documents other than the regulations (which may be or include codes or parts of codes of practical guidance issued or approved by the Secretary of State)".

Regulation 19 of the Weights and Measures (Packaged Goods) Regulations 1979 implements this by saying:

> "The provisions of the Packers' Code specified . . . below shall have effect for the purposes of determining questions as to the matters specified . . ."

As the introduction to the code itself explains,

> ". . . the Code is in effect an extension of the Regulations, or rather an amplification of them and, as such, has statutory significance . . . It is stressed, however, that the greater part of the Code is advisory, although nothing precludes any of it from being referred to in court proceedings, by the prosecution or the defence. Because of the legal status of those parts of the Code which are listed in the 1979 Regulations, the Code is referred to specifically, by title and date of issue, in the Regulations. Thus, no part of the Code can be changed without the introduction of a new Statutory Instrument, which requires Parliamentary approval."

Somewhat similar provisions are found in sections 16 and 17 of the Health and Safety at Work etc. Act 1974. The Health and Safety Commission are empowered to issue codes of practice for providing practical guidance with respect to the basic safety provisions of the Act. But—unlike the provisions in the Weights and Measures Act 1979—the codes do not actually have the force of law, although they can be referred to in civil and criminal proceedings.

Likewise, section 13 (8) of the Food and Drugs Act 1955 requires government Ministers to

> ". . . take such steps as they think expedient for publishing codes of

practice in connection with [food hygiene] for the purpose of giving advice
and guidance to persons responsible for compliance . . ."

Similarly, section 10 of the Insurance Brokers (Registration) Act
1977, under the heading 'Code of Conduct' requires the Insurance
Brokers Registration Council, set up by the Act, to

". . . draw up . . . a statement of the acts and omissions which . . . in particular circumstances, constitute in the opinion of the Council unprofessional
conduct",

The crunch comes in section 15, which gives the Disciplinary
Committee of the Council power to erase the name of a registered
insurance broker from its list on the grounds, among other things, of
having been 'guilty of unprofessional conduct'. Here, therefore, is
another kind of legal sanction for non-compliance with a code.

Another solution may well lie in having a middle system of law,
whereby an infringement of a code of practice would give rise to
liability to a civil penalty. The requirement for precision of language
and rigid procedures, rightly demanded in criminal provisions, need
not apply to a system which, by definition, is not part of the criminal
law, and yet is able to impose sanctions for acts unlawful by law.

There has been considerable discussion in recent years about
advertising controls, and an EEC draft Directive on this subject has
caused much debate on the extent to which it is appropriate to control advertising practices by law, as distinct from leaving control
within codes of practice. The alternative to controlling advertising,
or at least a substantial part of it, through a middle system of law,
has not been considered.

In practice this would be little different from the disciplines currently imposed on the industry through the codes, with the important exception that those people and things currently outside the
codes (doorstep salesmen and point of sale material, for instance)
would be subject to effective sanctions. And consumer organisa-
tions, who have been calling for some kind of statutory back-up for
advertising codes, would presumably be satisfied to see these codes
given the force of law, even though it would not be the criminal law.

Current legislative policy

While the theoretical basis for a civil penalty as the sanction for unlawful behaviour of a relatively minor character exists in our legal system, a search through current statutes would show that its use is, to put it mildly, somewhat out of fashion. A glance at some of the statutes passed in 1979 shows that, overwhelmingly, Parliament plumbs in favour making unlawful behaviour a criminal offence, even though the offence is often trivial in character, and often no criminal intent is demanded.

Customs and Excise Management Act 1979

This is a consolidating measure, so its legislative philosophy cannot be taken as necessarily indicative of the general approach in 1979. It is useful in showing, however, that one statute can contain a myriad of offences, most of which do not appear to require any criminal intention. It is also worth noting that in this Act the word 'penalty' is frequently used, but only in the context of creating a criminal offence. The most common form of wording is something like this:

> "Any person who (does something prohibited) . . . shall be liable on summary conviction to a penalty of £. . .".

The use of the word 'conviction' shows that Parliament intended such section to create criminal offences.

It is also interesting to note that the legislation governing liability for, and collection of, customs and excise duties contrasts strongly with income tax and capital taxes. The former uses the criminal law, the latter the middle system of law. There does not seem to be any logical reason for this distinction, except that in the case of customs and excise duties the magistrates court has been the traditional forum for enforcement, whereas with income tax and the other taxes collected by the Inland Revenue, separate tribunals, the commissioners for the general purposes of the income tax—commonly known as the general commissioners—have had jurisdiction.

Section 78 of the Customs and Excise Act 1979 provides the sanction for the legal obligation with which the average citizen is most familiar: the duty to declare things bought abroad when arriving at an airport or sea port:

"Any person failing to declare any thing . . . as required by this section shall be liable *on summary conviction* to a penalty of three times the value of the thing not declared . . . or £100 . . . whichever is the greater."

Agricultural Statistics Act 1979

The Act is also a consolidating measure. Its interest lies in the differing degrees of culpability provided for in section 4, under the heading 'Penalties'. The Act requires farmers and others to provide information to the government about the use of agricultural land and similar matters, so that the Ministry of Agriculture and Food may know what is going on.

Section 4 (1) says:

"Any person who without reasonable excuse fails to furnish information in compliance with a requirement under section 1 or 2 above shall be liable on summary conviction to a fine not exceeding £50".

Section 4 (2) says:

"If any person . . .
in purported compliance with a requirement imposed under section 1 or 2 above knowingly or recklessly furnishes any information which is false in any material particular . . . he shall be liable on summary conviction to imprisonment for a term not exceeding 3 months or to a fine not exceeding [£1000] or to both, or on conviction on indictment to imprisonment for a term not exceeding 2 years or to a fine or to both".

The lesser offence under subsection 1 of failing to furnish information is only committed when it is done 'without reasonable excuse'. This is largely a question of fact, although ignorance of the statutory requirement is not likely to be taken as a reasonable excuse. It does, however, amount to a form of intention, and shows that, in this context, Parliament stopped short of making such failure an offence of strict liability.

If the opportunity had been given to the legislature, the sanction for failing to furnish information might well have been a civil penalty. If so, is it not likely that the section would have provided as the penalty a sum considerably in excess of £50? It would also have been easier to make it a matter of strict liability.

It is quite understandable that it was considered inappropriate to use the criminal law, with strict liability, for something which many citizens (especially farmers, perhaps) would regard as a piece of interfering bureaucracy. And yet the need for the state to have reliable information about UK agricultural land is also understandable. Given that, how else could such information be procured under statutory powers?

The answer—or at least *an* answer—lies surely in imposing the duty to provide information under the sanction of a civil penalty. This must be more sensible than making it a crime. And once the legislature escapes the necessity of using the criminal sanction, it is likely to be more relaxed about making the matter one of strict liability. In this way, the escape route for the not too conscientious citizen is blocked, or at least reduced. In addition, the legislature could feel more at ease in imposing a higher financial penalty, one which could make the average farmer sit up and take notice a bit more.

When one comes to subsection (2), an offence is only committed where information which is materially false is given knowingly or recklessly. Few would quarrel with that being a crime. At any rate *mens rea* is demanded.

If Parliament were minded to recast the sanctions under this statute in such a way as to import a civil penalty for the lesser offence, and still preserve the criminal character for the more serious offence, it would perhaps read like this:

> "(1) Any person who fails to furnish information in compliance with a requirement under section 1 or 2 shall be liable to a civil penalty not exceeding £250.
>
> (2) Any person who, in purported compliance with a requirement imposed under 1 or 2 above, knowingly or recklessly furnishes any information which is false in any material particular, shall be guilty of a criminal offence, and shall be liable on summary conviction to imprisonment for a term not exceeding 3 months or to a fine not exceeding £1000 or to both . . ."

Estate Agents Act 1979

This Act has introduced a novel means of seeking to control the activities of commerce: the concept of negative licensing. The philosophy is that anyone can carry on an estate agency business, but anyone who does so in a way which shows that he is unfit to be an estate agent can be forbidden to continue in business. Section 3 lays down a number of situations, including being convicted of offences involving fraud, and committing racial or sexual descrimination in relation to estate agency work, which can give rise to an estate agent being prohibited from continuing to do estate agency work.

Here, then, is a new approach to the middle ground of law—the area which straddles the criminal and civil legal systems. Once again one finds Parliament floundering somewhat uncertainly between the concepts available under existing legal systems. They rejected positive licensing of the kind adopted in the Consumer Credit Act 1974, on the grounds that it would not be appropriate to establish another complex, expensive, bureaucratic structure. It was recognised, on the other hand, that it would be difficult to specify in legislative language precisely all the things that estate agents should and should not do. So the new idea of negative licensing was enacted. It remains to be seen how successful it will be.

Negative licensing does not provide a substitute for the middle system of law, here advocated. It demonstrates, however, the established need to cover the middle ground between the familiar concepts of the criminal and the civil law—by some appropriate means.

Elsewhere in the Estate Agents Act 1979 are found examples of the use of criminal and civil sanctions. In some instances it is arguable that the use of a civil penalty might have been more appropriate. One example is in section 21. This requires an estate agent to disclose any personal interest he has in a property to any person with whom he embarks on negotiations with regard to the disposal or acquisition of that property. Subsection (6) says:

> "Failure by an estate agent to comply with any of the preceding provisions of this section may be taken into account by the Director in accordance with section 3 (1) (c) above but shall not render the estate agent liable to any criminal penalty nor constitute a ground for any civil claim".

In other words, the negative licensing provisions could be invoked against an estate agent who failed to disclose a personal interest in a transaction in which he was involved, so that he would be forbidden by the Director General of Fair Trading to carry on business as an estate agent. Beyond that, there is no sanction, neither criminal nor civil. This means that an estate agent can get away at least once with failing to disclose a conflict of interest. If Parliament considered that it was necessary to have a sanction, it could have said that failure to disclose an interest would render the estate agent liable to a civil penalty, as well as making him liable to the negative licensing procedure under section 3. No doubt the reason why they did not do so is that nobody thought of it.

Section 27 deals with 'obstruction and personation of authorised officers', that is, in effect, trading standards officers whose job will be to enforce the Estate Agents Act, to make sure for example, that estate agents are properly insured against loss of monies which they hold (such as deposits), and are keeping clients' monies in a bank account separate from their own monies.

Section 27 makes it a criminal offence if a person 'wilfully obstructs an authorised officer'. That is fair enough. But it then goes on to make it a criminal offence if a person 'without reasonable cause fails to give an authorised officer other assistance or information he may reasonably require in performing his functions under this Act'.

This surely is going too far. To make it a crime to fail to give an enforcement officer assistance or information is excessive, although it is not untypical of modern legislative trends. Obviously, those who do something active, which obstructs the reasonable investigation and enforcement of the law, should not be allowed to get away with it. But passive failure to provide help or information is another matter. There must be a better way of ensuring that people provide help and information than saying it is a crime if you do not. There is indeed a better way: to provide in such a case that a person should become liable to a civil penalty.

This is an excellent example of the unnecessary use of the criminal law as a sanction in a place of legislation. Because the draftman could think of nothing better, he makes it a crime. In section 21, he was dealing with estate agents' behaviour, so the sanction under the negative licensing procedure, approximating to the middle system, could be invoked: being forbidden from engaging in estate agency work. In section 27, the prohibition has to apply to 'any person', and accordingly that sanction will not work. A civil penalty would have been a more appropriate sanction under section 27 for failing to give assistance or information.

Those in favour

The first public reference to the idea of adopting in the UK a middle system of law seems to have been made rather casually at the annual conference of the Institute of Trading Standards Administration at Blackpool in June 1977, in a session on 'What the consumer really needs'. The Institute's Monthly Review (Vol 85, No 9) reported as follows:

> "Finally, he [David Tench, the Consumers' Association's legal officer] included a radical thought—a new kind of legal control. He suggested the time had come to stop using criminal law as the main basis of controlling the activities of traders. How much longer could they go on making behaviour which was not really wicked, criminal? . . . The time had come to take away from criminal law a great measure of consumer protection law. What we needed was a new 'medium-way', neither criminal nor civil but something in between. A great part of Weights and Measures, Food and Drugs and consumer safety law should be shifted into this new middle system of law whereby behaviour was controlled perhaps in shoppers or market courts where the sanctions were not fines but penalty procedures, involving inquiries not prosecutions, ending in decisions not convictions and orders not sentences. Our legal system had made some progress in Part 3 of the Fair Trading Act, but we needed urgently to re-think the legal system and introduce a new middle way suited to consumer affairs."

Retail Trading-Standards Association

In November 1978, support for the concept was expressed on behalf of the RTSA. The views of this organisation command particular respect, because its members included many important companies in the retailing world, including the House of Fraser, Selfridges, Heals, Debenhams, John Lewis, Boots, British Home Stores and Littlewoods, as well as Courtaulds and ICI from industry. Introducing the Association's annual report, its chairman, Mr Garvin Fisher, said:

> ". . . Unless legislation can be seen to be necessary, it is derided and disrespected and those who have to enforce it share the same disrespect. Our members do not obey the law because they are afraid of getting caught, but because they respect it. In fact, as legislation proliferates and enforcement officers get more work piled on them, the chances of getting caught if we do break the law get smaller.
>   We intend to seek out allies to work towards a 'middle system' of law. This is a concept that has already been floated by Consumers' Association

who certainly want undesirable market practices to be controlled. We recognise the difficulties of change but at the very least we think serious consideration should be given to a system where some of the 'offences' created by regulation should be treated as 'civil' offences in the magistrates courts and remove the stigma of 'crime' from acts of omission or the use of banned words which do not cause consumers economic or other detriment."

Association of Mail Order Publishers

In July 1979, the AMOP gave its support to the idea. The editorial in its official organ, AMOP News, said this:

"In times gone by it was sufficient and was generally accepted that some matters were criminal and some civil. Cattle stealing was a crime while trespass fitted acceptably into civil law . . . A division like this works well enough in a simple society, unencumbered by technology. Yet in modern society we try to control technology by law, and use the divisions of a pastoral society when deciding how to bring an offender to book. A breach of a Regulation is a crime: hence, a business man who transgresses the credit regulations by, say, omitting the true rates of interest, is a criminal, just like a horse thief.

The present state of affairs offends common sense. What is needed is a third category, mid-way between criminal and civil law. Within would be found all those offences, and there are a great many, which are at present technically crime. Commission of one of them should not be a crime but a civil wrong . . ."

Rt Hon Sally Oppenheim MP, Minister for Consumer Affairs

These sentiments received support from the Rt Hon Sally Oppenheim MP, Minister for Consumer Affairs. On 16 October 1979, when addressing the association whose views have just been quoted, she said:

"I am very conscious of the need to see whether the sanctions of consumer protection legislation can be made less offensive to the trading community without losing their efficacy.

Criminal measures sometimes seem unjust in the field of consumer protection but it is desirable from the viewpoint of traders as well as shoppers to act firmly against the recalcitrant and persistent offender. It can. however, seem too harsh to impose the same criminal penalties on the small trader who, while basically honest, may not be very well informed.

The radical way to change this position, which would require a thorough overhaul of the existing system of law, is by introducing a third system of law, a middle system, half-way between the civil and the criminal law.

The Association's newsletter recently took up this point and I was very impressed and encouraged to see it entering into these areas of debate: we need trade associations to participate fully in our deliberations."

After referring to the role of codes of practice, which she warmly supported, the Minister said:

"There is certainly something, if not everything, to be said for seeking an alternative to the criminal law for the extension of consumer protection in this country."

The Commercial Legislation Monitoring Group

A group from commerce and industry which is not at all friendly towards the consumer movement has also come out in favour of the middle system of law. In December 1979 a report was published by the Commercial Legislation Monitoring Group, a collection of miscellaneous interests mainly from industry, inspired by Mr Harry Shepherd from Marks & Spencer. The main burden of their report was directed, somewhat uncertainly, towards the alleged cost of consumer protection legislation. But towards the end of their report they said this:

"Criminal law should be retained for fraudulent practice, i.e. where there is proof of 'mens rea'. The possibility of a third system of law, neither civil nor criminal, should be further explored as being applicable to suitable consumer protection legislation, and we commend the initiative of the Minister of State at the Department of Trade in opening up discussion on this subject."

The Director General of Fair Trading

Mr Gordon Borrie, the Director General of Fair Trading, has also spoken of the present state of the law regarding consumer protection. While stopping short of full support for the middle system of law principle, he has at least spoken of it, and not against it. In a speech given to the Association of Law Teachers in March 1980, he described the growth of consumer protection law over the past 20 years. He referred to the legislation in the consumer field passed during that time. He went on to say:

> "... the new law had to be either civil or criminal ... the fundamental division of our law into civil law or criminal law remains as clear and unshaken in this area as in any other. The disadvantages of what I might call this rigid duopoly and the recent calls for a middle way or a middle system of law I will speak about later."

Later he said this:

> "It will be interesting to see these proposals worked out more fully. The proposals have much merit if they remove the resentment that so many traders feel against regulatory offences being part of the criminal law.
>
> On the other hand, it may be said that the law would lose much of its deterrent effect if it was taken outside the criminal calendar and enforcement consisted at least in part of arrangements made behind closed doors and never made public."

In effect, the crucial decisions are already made behind closed doors, namely the decisions about who should be prosecuted, and on what basis. A middle system of law would bring a good deal (but not all) of that aspect of enforcement into the open. It would seem also that Gordon Borrie's objections lie primarily in the suggestion that in operating the middle system of law, cases might be disposed of by agreement, without proceedings. This is part of the proposal as here argued, but it is not, of course, a requirement of the system. It would be perfectly possible to have a middle system of law which required that civil penalties could only be awarded by a court, and not be disposed of without proceedings.

In Parliament

The first time that the concept of a middle system of law was discussed in Parliament was in November 1979, during the consideration of the Competition Bill in Committee. Mr John Fraser MP, Opposition front bench spokesman on consumer affairs, and Minister of State for Prices and Consumer Protection in the previous government, put down an amendment to the Bill with a view to introducing a civil penalty as the sanction for the infringement of one of the provisions of the Bill. It was in relation to the clause in the Bill dealing with traders who had been indulging in anti-competitive practices being able to give an undertaking to the Director General of Fair Trading to refrain from doing so in the future. The question had arisen as to the absence from the Bill of any sanction for failure to honour such an undertaking. The amendment—inspired by Consumers' Association—was put down by Mr Fraser and read as follows:

> "(9) If any person who has given an undertaking under this section fails to carry it out, he shall be liable in civil proceedings brought by the Director in the Restrictive Practices Court:
> (a) to a penalty not exceeding £5000, and
> (b) if the failure continues after it has been declared by the court to a further penalty not exceeding £100 for each day on which the failure so continues."

Speaking to a standing committee of the House of Commons in support of this amendment on 27 November 1979, Mr Fraser said it

> ". . . would introduce a course of action which is absent from much of our law—a middle course of penalties which do not involve criminal sanctions. The amendments provide for the court to be able to exact a penalty which is not a criminal penalty. I know that the right hon. Lady has referred already to such matters but there is a case for the Government as a whole to look into a middle system of law for the enforcement of administrative provisions which does not involve criminal penalties.
>
> There are a number of laws which protect consumers. The Unfair Contract Terms Act and the Supply of Goods (Implied Terms) Act are purely civil Acts. Other laws which protect consumers, such as the Weights and Measures Act and the Consumer Safety Act are purely criminal Acts. The Consumer Credit Act has administrative provisions similar to those in the Bill. Licensing is an administrative sanction. There are criminal sanctions for failure to abide by the law, and civil sanctions for non-enforcability of credit agreements. The Consumer Credit Act is a mixture of administrative, civil and criminal sanctions.
>
> Under this legislation there will be some criminal sanctions because if, at the end of the day, an order is made against a firm, and that firm breaches the terms of the order, a criminal sanction will obtain, and a fine will be payable. But should the Government rely so heavily upon criminal sanctions? I feel that if we try to introduce new consumer or competition legislation, and if we impose a criminal sanction, industry is more likely to resist the imposition of new intervention in competition on consumer matters because it contains a criminal penalty. That is the first difficulty.
>
> Secondly, the introduction of criminal penalties tends to devalue the criminal law. That is abundantly apparent in the case of many minor motoring offences. Parking restrictions would not be accepted if they always involved people ending up in a criminal court. Because the penalty is usually a £6 fine, people find that acceptable. Perhaps there should be a mere civil penalty for breach of orders as regards the Bill. That must be

looked at by the Department of Trade in conjunction with other Departments, including the Lord Chancellor's Department.

Inadequate consideration has been given to the sanction that is to be imposed for breach of orders. We have an opportunity to put into the Bill a mere penalty arrangement. It would not involve criminal proceedings, and would be exacted by the Restrictive Practices Court.

The right of civil action has a precedent and is important. The second provision in the amendment is unprecedented, but that does not devalue its importance. It deserves serious attention not merely by the Department of Trade but by other Departments as well."

Speaking in support of the amendment, Mr Fraser's colleague on the Labour side, Mr Ioan Evans MP, said:

"We have in evidence the views expressed by the Consumers' Association. It has said that it is not satisfied that the sanctions provided by the Bill for non-compliance with its provisions are adequate. No sanction is provided in the Bill for failure by a company to observe an undertaking given under clause 4. The only remedy open to the Director General of Fair Trading for such failure would be to initiate a reference to the Monopolies and Mergers Commission under clause 5. The association says that it would then become necessary for the relatively cumbersome procedure laid down in that clause to be invoked. A company in breach of its undertaking would, in fact, be in no different position from a company from whom no undertaking at all had been obtained and in respect of whose conduct clause 5 would apply. It adds:

'We consider that some sanction should operate against a company which fails to honour a solemn undertaking to the Director to discontinue what would amount to an admitted non-competitive practice.'

I think the Committee will recognise that the Consumers' Association has done a tremendous job for consumer protection. It brings out the 'Which?' publication. It is now joining my honourable Friend and myself in saying that there should be some sanction.

The sanction, as my hon. Friend has said, should be a civil penalty on the lines widely applied in tax legislation. It would be an innovation in competition law. It would introduce a sanction on the lines of a middle system of law. The right hon. Lady, speaking in a different context on October 16—on whether sanctions in consumer protection legislation could be made less offensive to the trading community without losing their efficacy—said:

'The radical way to change this position, which would require a thorough overhaul of the existing system of law, is by introducing a third system of law, a middle system, halfway between the civil and the criminal law.'

I hope that the Committee will today make further progress and that a strengthening of this clause will be accepted by the right hon. Lady in the form of these amendments."

The Minister's reply was as follows:

"The hon. Member for Norwood (Mr Fraser) and the hon. Member for Aberdare (Mr Evans) propose to impose heavy penalties for breach of undertakings. That we would not wish to condone. It would be unreasonable and unjustified to impose this type of penalty at this stage. As the hon. Member for Aberdare has said, there is a sanction already in referral to the Monopolies and Mergers Commission. The hon. Gentleman's amendment No. 121 would have the effect of discriminating against firms that gave undertakings as opposed to those which did not give undertakings and wanted the Monopolies and Mergers Commission investigation. The comparison with part III of the Fair Trading Act is inappropriate in this respect. If a case is referred to the Restrictive Practices Court, that is not a penalty for breach of an undertaking but the normal procedure for determining whether a trader is guilty of a course of conduct detrimental to the consumer interest.

A breach of an undertaking may not be premeditated. It may be inadvertent. It would be wrong to impose heavier sanctions at that point. In relation to new clause 9, I would point out that if an undertaking that has been given is breached, it can be referred to the Monopolies and Mergers Commission. I take the point of the hon. Member for Aberdare that a firm would be no better off if it had not given an undertaking at that point. That is a valid argument. I cannot possibly accept his new clause.

We have tried to maintain a balance between what is fair in this respect. However, I will undertake, without giving any commitment that anything will follow, to look at the matter again because the hon. Member for Norwood makes a fair point."

As a consequence, Mr Fraser's amendment was withdrawn.

The Minister's non-committal reply is entirely reasonable in the context of that particular Bill, although it is somewhat in contrast to her earlier robust support for the principle of the middle system of law. Nobody seriously expected the Government to accept the introduction into our legal system of such a fundamental reform as an afterthought tacked on to a Bill dealing with competition. Nevertheless, it was a notable milestone: the idea of a middle system of law was in specific terms floated in Parliament for the first time; and Mr Fraser's support for the principle, which is probably echoed elsewhere in the House of Commons, is an important advance.

Justice

In 1980, Justice—the British section of the International Commission of Jurists—published a report entitled 'Breaking the Rules', after five years of research.

The first task the committee of Justice undertook was to try to define and classify all offences making up the criminal law in England and Wales. They found this very difficult. There is no published list of things which are forbidden by the criminal law. The Justice report therefore recommended that:

> ". . . an appropriate government department should publish as soon as possible, and thereafter keep up to date, a complete list of all criminal offences . . . known to the law, containing the definition of the ingredients of each offence, its source in statute or regulation, its mode of trial, its maximum penalties, and any special features . . ."

There being no such publication available at the moment, Justice—greatly daring—decided to commission research on this matter themselves, with a view to producing a list of all offences. The result is summarised as an appendix to their report. They found that the criminal law consists of a total of 7208 offences, created by 466 statutes and 37 statutory instruments. Of the crimes thus found, more than half—3747 according to their research—require no criminal intent, that is to say they are offences of strict liability. These 3747 offences form the raw material for the reforms they suggest. They are likewise the raw material for the middle system of law.

Justice examines the options for reforming the system. The report advocates drawing a distinction between crimes on the one hand and what it calls 'contraventions' on the other. Justice says that large sections of the criminal law should be 'decriminalised', but that in each case the behaviour in question should continue to be prohibited by law by becoming a contravention, subject to a penalty.

There is a good deal of common ground between the Justice report and the idea of a middle system of law. The basic philosophy is the same. Some quotations from the Justice report will demonstrate this:

> ". . . drawing a formal distinction between crimes and contraventions in English law would go some way towards increasing respect for the remaining truly criminal part of that law, and that would be an important benefit. Such a reform would therefore not be merely cosmetic, and we believe

that it should be undertaken in any event. It is, in any case, the condition precedent for any further steps along this road.

That first step would require legislation, but of an essentially simple kind. What would be necessary would be one or more Acts declaring that, on and after the appointed day, the offences listed in the Schedule to the Act shall cease to be criminal offences and shall become contraventions . . .

In future legislation, Parliament would need to apply its mind specifically to the question whether new categories of conduct to be regulated should be made crimes or contraventions, and provide accordingly.

Without more than this, all the rest of the existing apparatus for enforcing regulations would remain unchanged. Contraventions would continue to be prosecuted by whoever prosecutes them now . . . ; they would come before the same courts (in virtually all cases, the Magistrates' Courts); . . . and they would continue to attract the same penalties as they do now. But at least the contravening citizen would no longer suffer the stigma of being prosecuted and tried for a crime, convicted of a crime, and acquiring (or adding to) a criminal record—and that, in our view, would be a substantial and valuable step forward.

Is it feasible, at the present time, to go further than this, and begin to move towards the second step—that is, a different procedure for imposing penalties for contraventions which will not always and necessarily involve the criminal courts? We think it might be."

The middle system of law would go further than the Justice solution. It would not merely decriminalise much of the criminal law, but would provide a separate procedure for imposing civil penalties for what Justice describes as 'contraventions'. There are differences of emphasis and of language in the way Justice analyses and describes the problem. The most significant difference lies in the approach of Justice to the function of administrative agencies.

Justice envisages that a contravention of the law (which has become decriminalised) should be dealt with administratively by the agency charged with its enforcement. Paragraph 4.12 of the Justice report envisages that an agency itself should, in the first instance, be able to impose a penalty, with the option for the alleged contravenor to have the matter referred to the magistrates court.

The middle system of law approach would achieve a similar result by different means. The administrative agency would be free to start proceedings for a civil penalty, or to negotiate a settlement with the suspected contravenor. If no agreement were reached, the matter would have to be referred to the court.

Justices Clerks' Society

In May 1981, the Justices Clerks' Society published a report entitled 'Decriminalisation—An Argument for Reform'. It made recommendations broadly similar to those advocated by Justice. It supported the view that existing offences should become categorised as 'crimes' or 'contraventions', the latter constituting substantially the same body of law as that covered by the middle system of law. The Society argued:

> ". . . a large section of the population does not regard most of the recently created offences as 'crimes'. The view is growing that these offences are not indicative of the sort of evil of mind that justifies criminal prosecution. Most regard such offences as mere 'contraventions', deserving of penalty but not the stigma of a criminal conviction."

The Justices Clerks' Society report lists the kinds of offences which should continue to be crimes, and those which might become contraventions. Among the offences which it considers should remain crimes are 'Offences that cause economic damage to other persons, e.g. offences under the Trade Descriptions Act'. This contrasts with the view expressed here, that some consumer law offences, including those under the Trade Descriptions Act, could well merit being decriminalised and absorbed into the proposed middle system of law.

No doubt justices clerks would, on the whole, agree that there is much scope for debate on what offences merit changing their character, and no two advocates of a new system would entirely agree as to the list of suitable candidates. There is complete agreement, however, as to the need for a new system.

The proposals of the Justices Clerks' Society differ in several respects from the Justice proposals, and from what is suggested here. The Society draws a distinction between penalties imposed by enforcing agencies, and which are exacted for the non-payment of money, and penalties to be paid by way of fixed penalty, based on the present fixed penalty procedure under the Road Traffic Acts. There may well be some merit in such a distinction, but it is perhaps a matter best left to evolve as part of the new system, rather than something to be imposed from the outset.

Probably the most compelling part of the argument put forward by the Justices Clerks' Society is their compilation of the number of offences dealt with in magistrates courts in England and Wales in

1979 'for offences that are appropriate for decriminalisation'. Of the total of 1,588,541 people proceeded against for all summary offences in that year, 1,234,909 (77 per cent) were prosecuted for offences which, even on a conservative view of the matter, should not be criminal offences at all. Of these, by far the greater number— 1,089,073—were for motoring offences. The report demonstrates convincingly the financial and other benefits that could be derived from removing so massive a proportion of cases from the imbroglio of criminal law procedure.

The options
The reports of Justice and of the Justices Clerks' Society command great respect. They are valuable contributions to the debate on the extent to which the present legal system meet the needs of society in the last two decades of the 20th century. There are no doubt other options open to improve the present unsatisfactory situation. Other ideas will no doubt be put forward.

Eventually Parliament will have to decide.

How it would work

If Parliament were to decide to expand the role of civil penalties, how would they set about the task?

It should be in new laws, in planning future legislation, that opportunities to use a civil penalty as a sanction should be considered. The way forward would probably lie in cautious experimentation, at least at first. It would be important not to rush headlong into legislating for civil penalties in Bills not really suited for this treatment. It would be particularly important that the proposal should not go off at half cock, by being tried out in unsuitable circumstances.

It would be a mistake to begin by considering first what offences may be removed from the criminal calendar. Only when a system of civil penalties has been running for several years, and has been shown to be acceptable and effective, should there be any question of decriminalising existing offences in our law. The same applies to transferring controls at present within the civil law. At first, only new controls that are mooted should be the candidates for the middle system.

Privacy and data protection

An example of the sort of new legislation that might be suitable for this treatment is that dealing with privacy, and in particular the proposals of the Lindop report, dealing with data protection. The report recommends the establishment of legal controls on the use of computerised information. It rejects (para 19.18) reliance on the civil law only as an adequate system of control. Instead, the report recommends codes of practice, backed by statutory controls. It also recommends that a government agency be established to supervise the necessary controls, including maintaining a register of data users. The agency would be called the Data Protection Authority (DPA). In relation to both aspects, the Lindop report suggests that non-compliance with the requirements of the law should be a criminal offence. Para 19.89 of the Lindop report says:

> "19.89. Under the scheme which we propose there would be two main criminal offences: failure to register a registrable activity, and breach of a Code of Practice."

This is very much middle system of law territory. Few would quarrel with the general approach of the Lindop report—that legal controls are needed to protect people from unwarranted invasions of their privacy through the development of computerised data systems. But the Lindop report reveals classic symptoms of anguishing between the civil and criminal legal systems and failing to come up with an appropriate answer.

A civil penalty would be the most appropriate sanction for much of the regulatory law which the report proposes. A civil penalty is peculiarly appropriate as the sanction for breach of the codes of practice, which the Lindop report suggests as the main safeguard for the citizen.

Development

Once the middle system of law has been launched, it may be expected to gather momentum quickly. Each Bill before Parliament would be scrutinised as to the kind of sanctions it seeks to impose. Ministers, civil servants and MPs could be encouraged to ask: must this be made an offence? Would not a civil penalty do? The plethora of regulatory legislation which is now an inescapable characteristic of all parliamentary sessions could provide fertile ground for the emerging middle system of law. In time, in legislation dealing with matters which are not criminal in any real sense, the civil penalty might become the rule, rather than the exception.

Transfers from existing civil law
As the system develops, it will become possible to transfer to it some of the legislation at present uncomfortably accommodated in the civil law. In particular, the law about discrimination and competition law seem appropriate candidates: their sanctions could be strengthened by the imposition of civil penalties for their breach.

Transfers from the existing criminal law
Finally, when the middle system of law is established, a start can be made on the most important sector of all: the gradual process of removing from the criminal law the mass of regulatory offences which would be more appropriately dealt with by the new system.

A Civil Penalties Act

At some stage in the evolution of the new system, it will be found necessary to enact comprehensive provisions. At that stage there will have to be enacted a Civil Penalties Act. This will be the point at which the middle system of law reaches maturity. It should not be enacted until there has been enough time to get the feel of the new system in practice. The Civil Penalties Act will lay down the criteria on which the new system will thereafter work: which courts to have jurisdiction, what mental elements to be required in proceedings for civil penalties, the relevance of negligence, the defences that may be pleaded, who may bring proceedings, the form of such proceedings, the burden of proof, the means of enforcement, the right to settle proceedings (or as the case may be), the question of costs, and the power to make compensation orders (or not, as Parliament may decide).

The language of the middle system

It is legitimate to guess at some of the words that may come to be used in operating the new system. It is important that appropriate language should be used in relation to the middle system, so that it can acquire a distinct character and flavour of its own.

Thus, where the civil law speaks of a *tort*, a *breach of contract* or a *breach of trust*, and the criminal law speaks of a *crime* or an *offence*, the middle system will speak of a *contravention*, an *infringement*, a *transgression* or an *infraction*. *Illegal* is a word which should be preserved for use in relation to the criminal law; *unlawful* is the more appropriate word to use in relation to the middle system, even though it is also used (and will continue to be used) in relation to the civil law.

Liable and *liability* are words appropriate to all three systems. But *penalty* ought to become a word used exclusively in the middle system, and where it is used under existing legislation (as in the

Customs and Excise Management Act 1979, referred to earlier under 'Current Legislative Policy') it ought to be phased out. In no circumstances should the words *crime* or *criminal*, or *offence* or *guilty* be used in relation to the middle system. *Penalty, liability, contravention, transgression* and *violation* are all appropriate for use in the middle system, unlike *fine, imprisonment, prosecute* and *charge*.

An authority having the responsibility of enforcing a law covered by the middle system would *sue* for a civil penalty, which would be said to be *forfeited* or made *payable* by the *defendant* (or perhaps *respondent*), to the *complaint* or *summons*.

The key word is *penalty*. Until that word has been phased out of use in the criminal law (which is going to take many years), it would be better to speak of a *civil* penalty, to emphasise its use in the new sense.

The framing of statutory sanctions

The model for future use should be the precedent set in tax law by the Taxes Management Act. Section 93 of that Act has already been quoted; its essence illustrates the way future statutes might be worded:

> "If any person has been required by any notice . . . to deliver any return, and he fails to comply with the notice he shall be liable . . . to a penalty not exceeding . . . £50 . . ."

Change that to 'a civil penalty' and there is the precedent.

The language used in the Electric Lighting (Clauses) Act 1899, also quoted earlier, is on the same lines:

> "Whenever the Undertakers make default in supplying energy . . . they shall be liable in respect of default to a penalty not exceeding forty shillings . . ."

Again, all that needs to be changed is that it should be a *civil* penalty.

The clause put forward when the Competition Bill was in Committee in the House of Commons in November 1979 was:

> "If any person who has given an undertaking . . . fails to carry it out, he shall be liable in civil proceedings brought by the Director in the Restrictive Practices Court . . . to a penalty not exceeding £5,000 . . ."

There, the civil nature of the penalty is emphasised by saying 'in civil proceedings', as that was the whole point of the amendment. It would have been equally appropriate to have said:

> ". . . shall be liable in proceedings brought by the Director in the Restrictive Practices Court . . . to a civil penalty . . ."

Codes

Codes of practice may be more difficult to deal with. In the case of a code inspired by the Office of Fair Trading under section 124 (3) of the Fair Trading Act 1973, it would be necessary to introduce provisions for enabling such a code to become an 'approved' code. It could be sufficient for the Director General of Fair Trading to approve it, or it might need to be the Secretary of State. One way or another, when a code would become approved and promulgated, it would then become subject to the enacted sanction. This might read as follows:

> "A person who fails to perform a duty imposed on him by an approved code of practice shall be liable in proceedings to a civil penalty . . ."

It might go on to say 'not exceeding £1000', or whatever figure Parliament might determine. In the early days of the new regime, it might be helpful to the courts if Parliament indicated in the legislation a range of penalty awards for various degrees of infringement. In due time, when things have settled down, and the courts become accustomed to awarding appropriate levels of penalties, it might be better to revert to the general formula of 'a civil penalty not exceeding £——', as with fines under the criminal law at present.

Discrimination

In the case of sex and race discrimination, Parliament will have to take a simple decision: should it be made *penal* (not criminal) to commit an unlawful act of discrimination?

At present, discrimination is a tort, but in the case of persistent acts of discrimination it can be stopped by injunction in civil proceedings brought at the behest of a government body, financed out of public funds. It is thus an unlawful civil wrong of a special character. If discrimination is to be forbidden, but not by the criminal law, the way to do so should be by imposing a civil penalty.

The existing provisions about civil proceedings by persons aggrieved in relation to unlawful discrimination ought to be retained, but there should be added a provision on these lines:

> "A person who commits an act of discrimination which is unlawful by virtue of this Act shall be liable in proceedings brought by the Commission to a civil penalty not exceeding £1,000".

The same could apply to sex discrimination. Provisions on these lines would add the necessary muscle to the present law on discrimination, bringing it effectively within the law by the threat of a financial penalty, but without making it a criminal offence. This would enhance the effectiveness of this sensitive branch of the law, without causing affront to those who strenuously resist the idea of discrimination being a crime.

Two tier approach

The main role of the middle system of law will eventually be to absorb those parts of the criminal law which are essentially regulatory in character. The raw material for this will be derived firstly from future legislation, and secondly from those parts of the present criminal code which are regulatory, which involve offences of strict liability.

In practice it might work out more subtly than that. In many areas of the law there are degrees of culpability. Because of the indiscriminate use of the criminal law as the sanction for acts forbidden by law, there is little scope under the present law for distinguishing these degrees of culpability. The only reflection of the degree of wrongfulness which Parliament ascribes to the acts forbidden is to be found in the maximum punishment permitted—imprisonment for a specified term or a fine of a certain sum, or both.

With the advent of the middle system of law, Parliament will be able to determine, in any particular area of social concern, that some acts are to be considered henceforth as wicked, and forbidden under the sanction of the criminal law, and other acts are considered to be not wicked, but in need of regulation, and so forbidden under the sanction of a civil penalty. It will, of course, be for Parliament to choose what goes in which category. The point is that there is no reason why the same statute should not use both systems, depending on the kinds of conduct Parliament seeks to bring within the law.

Broadly speaking, conduct involving *mens rea* (criminal intention) is likely to continue to be within the realm of the criminal law. So where the description of the proscribed behaviour includes words such as 'knowingly' or 'with intent to defraud' or expressions of that kind, it is likely that the criminal law will remain the sanction. Where no such words are included in the prohibition, and Parliament intends to impose strict liability, the middle system of law, with its civil penalty, will be the more appropriate.

Of course, in certain instances cases of strict liability will continue to be found in the criminal law, and cases where infringement demands an intention going with the forbidden act will be put into the middle system of law. But the general rule could well become that *mens rea* is usually required for crimes and none for the middle system.

On this basis, statutes may come to be reframed with sanctions on a two tier basis—some acts being made criminal, others made subject to a civil penalty. Take as an example the Trade Descriptions Act 1968, since that is probably the most familiar part of consumer law which could be dealt with in the way suggested. Section 1 (1) of the Act at present reads as follows:

> (1) Any person who, in the course of a trade or business—
> (a) applies a false trade description to any goods; or
> (b) supplies or offers to supply any goods to which a false trade description is applied;
> shall, subject to the provisions of this Act, be guilty of an offence.

This might be remodelled on the following lines:

> (1) No person shall in the course of a trade or business—
> (a) apply a false trade description to any goods; or
> (b) supply or offer to supply any goods to which a false trade description is applied.
> (2) A person who contravenes subsection (1) above shall forfeit a civil penalty.
> (3) A person who contravenes subsection (1) above and who knows or ought to know of the falsity of the trade description and does so with intent to defraud shall be guilty of an offence.

There is room for debate about the principles that should apply in relation to the suggested subsection (3). As drafted, both knowledge and intent to defraud are demanded. This need not be the case—one or the other could be demanded, instead of both. The point is that, in this context, at least one of them ought to be required when making it a criminal offence.

In real life, of course, a trading standards officer may suspect *mens rea*, but not be able to prove it. In such a case, he has the option of seeking further evidence in order to prove *mens rea* and then proceed for the crime, or proceed on the basis of seeking a civil penalty, and no more.

Pecuniary settlements

One of the important questions that will have to be decided in relation to the administration of the middle system is whether it will be lawful for an enforcement agency to deal with cases without having to take them all to court. In other words, whether out of court settlements will be possible, or whether—as with the criminal law—the rule will be that only courts can dispose of cases.

Under the fixed penalty procedure available for certain minor road traffic offences, there already exists a system of disposing of criminal offences by consent without legal proceedings. This shows that the walls do not come tumbling down if the state allows prohibited acts to be dealt with by procedures not involving courts.

Of course, it has always been possible to settle civil claims without going to court—even when proceedings in the civil courts have begun. So, out of court settlements should be allowed for the middle system. In the United States, this is possible, and has apparently worked without problems. Since the proceedings are civil, though penal, there seems to be no reason why the civil law philosophy in this respect should not prevail.

There would be great advantages in adopting this rule. In the first place, it may be foreseen that in the great majority of cases there would be no need for proceedings. Looking, for example, at the area of consumer law, one can imagine that a trading standards officer will no longer be faced with the alternatives of either letting an offending trader get away entirely with a breach of the law, or going through the rigmarole of bringing a prosecution (with all the time, expense and trouble which that involves). He will instead be able to negotiate with the trader about his willingness to dispose of the complaint by the payment of a civil penalty. If he is willing, they can negotiate as to the amount of the penalty, based on the amount that the parties would expect the court to award. This is what happens in regard to civil claims for damages under the present system. Obviously, if the parties cannot agree, either as to liability or as to the amount of the penalty, the matter will have to go to court. But it is likely that in the majority of cases, it will be possible to dispose of the matter by agreement. Of course, some procedural safeguards will be necessary. Appropriate notices will have to be given telling the individual of his right to have the matter taken to court, and underlining the voluntary nature of the compromise proposed.

Considerable public expense would be saved from cases which would no longer have to go to court, the public purse would greatly benefit by the inflow of civil penalties not only from cases taken to court but also from the outcome of investigations which, under the present system, give rise to no proceedings at all. Many offenders who at present get away scot free with having committed criminal offences would be made to atone by paying a penalty.

It is sometimes suggested that allowing compromises in this way would somehow open the door to the corruption of enforcement officers. The present system is equally, if not more, open to this objection. Whether offenders are prosecuted or not currently is very much a matter within the discretion of the enforcement officer. It is often a matter of degree, and of hit and miss, whether—in any particular case—a trader is prosecuted or not. Officers are not corrupted by this power that they already have. They do not take bribes for not prosecuting offenders in marginal cases. Neither would they if they were allowed to negotiate settlements out of court under the middle system of law. The money the wrongdoer agrees to pay would not be in cash, and handed over there and then. It would, like all public money, have to be properly handled and accounted for.

The system of out of court settlements works perfectly well in the area of Revenue law, and there is no reason why it should not work equally well elsewhere. It would add a new dimension to law enforcement. Far fewer people would get away without incurring any penalty, or with a mere warning, and enforcement officers would be able to demonstrate a greater effectiveness in the results of their case work.

However, the new system could operate quite well, even if it were to be a requirement that all claims for civil penalties should go to court. If Parliament were to feel uneasy on this score, the criminal law philosophy could be maintained at first, and an open mind kept by the legislature on the question of out of court settlements. In due time, once the middle system has gathered momentum, and is generally regarded as a success, the principle of out of court settlements could be introduced gradually.

The courts

Under English law, the administration of the civil and criminal legal systems is separate. Crown Courts and magistrates courts deal with the criminal law; the High Court and county courts deal with the civil law. Where would the middle system of law be administered?

There are several possibilities. Ideally, there would be a new court system designed to cater exclusively for the new system. This would have the advantage of demonstrating that the new system is entirely distinct from the existing ones. However, there is no prospect of Parliament sanctioning the establishment of a new court system, certainly not on the basis of a theory. Expense, not to mention bureaucracy, rules this out completely.

A variant on the concept of a new court system is the establishment of special courts, sector by sector. Thus it could be envisaged that, in the area of competition law and consumer affairs, there could be established a market court, on the lines of that in Sweden. Similarly, traffic courts might be set up to enforce those parts of the criminal law to be hived off from the existing criminal law.

This, in fact, is the arrangement which already exists for the one significant example of the middle system of law already operating: tax law. Penalties (let us remember to call them *civil* penalties) under the tax code are dealt with by the Taxes Management Act 1970, section 100. This says that penalty proceedings are generally brought before the General Commissioners of Income Tax, a tribunal established for the determination of disputes which arise in relation to tax matters. A body of local General Commissioners exists for every part of the country. They operate much like a local bench of JPs, except that they sit in private. They hear and determine tax appeals, and order penalties. In so doing, they act judicially—they are not an administrative tribunal. They are, to all intents and purposes, the court established by law to determine tax questions.

Penalty proceedings for infringements of the tax laws can also be brought in the High Court. The Crown Court, it should be noted, has no jurisdiction, which demonstrates that these penalty proceedings are essentially civil in nature. Indeed, section 100 of the Taxes Management Act 1970 says specifically that proceedings for penalties which are brought in the High Court are deemed to be civil proceedings by the Crown, within the meaning of the Crown Proceedings Act 1947. Tax courts administer the civil and the middle system of law side by side, quite happily.

In the current economic climate it is hardly likely that Parliament would agree to the setting up of special courts or tribunals to administer, sector by sector, those areas of the law ripe for adopting the middle system of law. The tax courts (in the form of the General Commissioners) are *sui generis*; even if there were merit in following the precedent from the tax field, it is simply not going to happen, certainly not on a significant scale. In any event, to do so would fragment the evolution of the middle system and prevent the development of the new system on a comprehensive and co-ordinated basis.

The middle system of law will therefore have to be handed over either to the existing civil or criminal courts. The civil courts are likely to respond to this new responsibility in a creative and sensible way. For a start, all civil courts have a lawyer in charge (although that is hardly a guarantee of an enlightened, let alone a radical, approach to administering justice). Their legal training gives rise to an understanding of the essential functions of the two systems we already have, and legal training will help in understanding the essential role of the third. Also, the civil courts have experience of branches of the law, such as race and sex discrimination, which (although technically within the civil law), are in reality part of that area of law which is in the middle.

The county court could readily absorb jurisdiction for administering the middle system. It might mean, in due course, an increased burden of work, but there should be a corresponding decrease in work in the magistrates courts.

However, the most appropriate forum for the middle system would be the magistrates court. The Crown Court could take the minority of cases which are serious or raise difficult points of law or principle.

There are disadvantages in giving the middle system to the criminal courts. It cannot be too often emphasised that the middle system is an entirely distinct system from the criminal system, so that it will not be a criminal offence to incur liability to a civil penalty. It may take a bit of time—perhaps even several generations—before this idea really sinks in. The award of a penalty, even if it is clearly labelled a civil penalty, is still going to be seen as much the same as a fine in a criminal case. The justices of the peace who will have to sit in judgement in cases arising under the middle system of law, the majority of whom are laymen, will continue to hand down justice in much the same way as that to which they are accustomed. They may take a long time to recognize that this is a new and different kind of justice, and that the criteria they have been applying in criminal cases do not apply to the new system, or—if they do—only in a different way. Ultimately, magistrates will realise that the cases they try under the middle system are different in kind, that they are administering a different animal from the criminal law, and that the people against whom they make awards of civil penalties are not criminals.

The main reason for conferring the middle system on the magistrates courts is that they are already there, and that they already have a considerable jurisdiction outside the criminal law. Their civil jurisdiction includes a large part of family law, including a large number of maintenance cases between wives and husbands. They also have a civil jurisdiction in relation to the collection of rates. Section 50 of the Magistrates Courts Act 1952 enables them to hear and determine complaints in cases which are not criminal, and to order payment of civil debts which are within their jurisdiction. Included among these are those few examples where civil penalties already exist.

Magistrates courts are in a position greatly to expand their role of administering the law regarding civil penalties. As new legislation is enacted which starts to prohibit behaviour without making it criminal, these courts will begin to get the feel of their new responsibility. In time, existing civil jurisdiction falling within the middle territory will be transferred to them. Eventually, a considerable slice of their current law, presently criminal, will be decriminalised, and continue to be administered by them no longer as part of the criminal law, but as part of their new middle system.

INDEX

Index

Table of cases